WORDS FROM THE BIBLE
ABOUT HEALING AND GROWTH

Be Well

Edited and designed by Ben Alex

scandinavia

BE WELL
WORDS FROM THE BIBLE ABOUT HEALING AND GROWTH

Published by Scandinavia Publishing House 2012
Scandinavia Publishing House
Drejervej 15,3, DK-2400 Copenhagen, NV
Denmark
E-mail: info@scanpublishing.dk
Web: www.scanpublishing.dk

Concept, editing and design by Ben Alex
All quotes from New International Version unless otherwise noted
Photo copyright © Dreamstime pages 5,18,42,57,58,70,97,98,100,106,112,120
Photo copyright © Janis Zroback pages 8,11,15,23,24,29,32,35,36,41,49,50,60,62,69,72,75,81,82,84,
87,92,102,111,114,117,122,127
Visit Janis at http://www.redbubble.com/people/paintability

Printed in China
ISBN 978 87 7132 047 3

Do not conform
to the pattern of this world,
but be transformed
by the renewing of
your minds.

Romans 12:2a

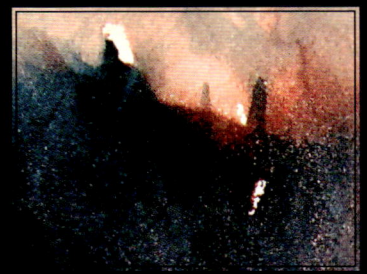

Have mercy on me, LORD,
for I am faint; heal me, LORD,
for my bones are in agony.

Psalm 6:2

If my people,
who are called by my name,
will humble themselves and pray and
seek my face and turn from their wicked ways,
then I will hear from heaven, and I will forgive
their sin and will heal their land.

2 Chronicles 7:14

nd healing

8

I said, "Have mercy
on me, LORD; heal me,
for I have sinned
against you."

Psalm 41:4

For he wounds,
but he also binds up;
he injures, but his
hands also heal.

Job 5:18

LORD my God,
I called to you for help,
and you healed me.

Psalm 30:2

If you listen carefully
to the LORD your God
and do what is right
in his eyes, if you pay
attention to his commands
and keep all his decrees,
I will not bring on you
any of the diseases
I brought on the Egyptians,
for I am the LORD,
who heals you.

Exodus 15:26

11

This is what the LORD says:
"I have healed this water.
Never again will it cause death
or make the land unproductive."

2 Kings 2:21

This is what the LORD,
the God of your father David, says:
"I have heard your prayer
and seen your tears;
I will heal you."

2 Kings 20:5b

"See now that
I myself am he!
There is no god besides me.
I put to death and I bring to life,
I have wounded and I will heal,
and no one can deliver
out of my hand."

Deuteronomy 32:39

And the LORD heard Hezekiah
and healed the people.

2 Chronicles 30:20

Praise the LORD, my soul,
and forget not all his benefits,
who forgives all your sins and
heals all your diseases.

Psalm 103:2-3

Your eye is the lamp of your body.
When your eyes are healthy, your whole body
also is full of light. But when they are unhealthy,
your body also is full of darkness.

Luke 11:34

He heals the brokenhearted
and binds up their wounds.

Psalm 147:3

He sent out his word and healed them;
he rescued them from the grave.

Psalm 107:20

The blind and the lame came to him
at the temple, and he healed them.

Matthew 21:14

Gracious words
are a honeycomb,
sweet to the soul and
healing to the bones.

Proverbs 16:24

The words of the reckless
pierce like swords, but the tongue
of the wise brings healing.

Proverbs 12:18

The centurion replied,
"Lord, I do not deserve to have you come under my roof.
But just say the word, and my servant will be healed."

Matthew 8:8

The moon will shine
like the sun, and the sunlight
will be seven times brighter,
like the light of seven full days,
when the LORD binds up
the bruises of his people
and heals the wounds
he inflicted.

Isaiah 30:26

But he was pierced for our transgressions,
he was crushed for our iniquities;
the punishment that brought us peace
was on him, and by his wounds we are healed.

Isaiah 53:5

Light in a messenger's eyes brings joy to the heart,
and good news gives health to the bones.

Proverbs 15:30

Strength

My son,
pay attention to what I say;
turn your ear to my words, for they are life
to those who find them and health
to one's whole body.

Proverbs 4:21-22

o the body

This will bring health to your body
and nourishment to your bones.

Proverbs 3:8

Lord, by such things people live;
and my spirit finds life in them too.
You restored me to health and let me live.

Isaiah 38:16

Fruit trees of all kinds
will grow on both banks of the river.
Their leaves will not wither, nor will their fruit fail.
Every month they will bear fruit, because the
water from the sanctuary flows to them.
Their fruit will serve for food and
their leaves for healing.

Ezekiel 47:12

Dear friend,
I pray that you may enjoy good health
and that all may go well with you,
even as your soul is getting along well.

3 John 1:2

Then your light will
break forth like the dawn,
and your healing will quickly appear;
then your righteousness will go before you,
and the glory of the LORD will
be your rear guard.

Isaiah 58:8

Come, let us return to the LORD.
He has torn us to pieces but he will heal us;
he has injured us but he will
bind up our wounds.

Hosea 6:1

Heal me, LORD,
and I will be healed;
save me and I will be saved,
for you are the one I praise.

Jeremiah 17:14

Say to him, "Long life to you!
Good health to you and your household!
And good health to all that is yours!"

1 Samuel 25:6

But for you
who revere my name,
the sun of righteousness
will rise with healing in its rays.
And you will go out and
frolic like well-fed calves.

Malachi 4:2

They did not realize
it was I who healed them.

Hosea 11:3

A large crowd followed him,
and he healed all who were ill.

Matthew 12:15b

Jesus brings

Jesus went throughout Galilee,
teaching in their synagogues,
proclaiming the good news of the kingdom,
and healing every disease and
sickness among the people.

Matthew 4:23

healing

When Jesus landed and saw
a large crowd, he had compassion
on them and healed their sick.

Matthew 14:14

33

She said to herself,
"If I only touch his cloak,
I will be healed."

Matthew 9:21

Immediately her bleeding stopped
and she felt in her body that she
was freed from her suffering.

Mark 5:29

Jesus turned and saw her.
"Take heart, daughter," he said,
"your faith has healed you."
And the woman was healed
at that moment.

Matthew 9:22

Jesus went through
all the towns and
villages, teaching in
their synagogues,
proclaiming the good
news of the kingdom
and healing every
disease and sickness.

Matthew 9:35

And wherever he went—
into villages, towns or countryside—
they placed the sick in the marketplaces.
They begged him to let them touch
even the edge of his cloak, and all
who touched it were healed.

Mark 6:56

37

People brought all their sick
to him and begged him to let the sick
just touch the edge of his cloak,
and all who touched it were healed.

Matthew 14:35-36

Jesus rebuked the demon,
and it came out of the boy,
and he was healed at that moment.

Matthew 17:18

Then he said to her,
"Daughter, your faith has healed you.
Go in peace."

Luke 8:48

Jesus said to him, "Receive your sight;
your faith has healed you."

Luke 18:42

He took her by the hand and said to her, "Talitha koum!"
(which means "Little girl, I say to you, get up!"). Immediately the girl stood up and began to walk around.

Mark 5: 41-42

But Jesus answered, "No more of this!"
And he touched the man's ear and healed him.

Luke 22:51

Then they brought him
a demon-possessed man
who was blind and mute,
and Jesus healed him,
so that he could both
talk and see.

Matthew 12:22

Then Jesus said to her,
"Woman, you have great faith!
Your request is granted."
And her daughter was healed
at that moment.

Matthew 15:28

While Jesus was
in one of the towns,
a man came along who
was covered with leprosy.
When he saw Jesus,
he fell with his face to the ground
and begged him, "Lord, if you are
willing, you can make me clean."
Jesus reached out his hand
and touched the man.
"I am willing," he said.
"Be clean!" And immediately
the leprosy left him.

Luke 5:12-13

"The Spirit of the Lord is on me,
because he has anointed me to proclaim
good news to the poor. He has sent me to
proclaim freedom for the prisoners and
recovery of sight for the blind,
to set the oppressed free...."
And laying his hands on
each one, he healed them.

Luke 4:18,40

The kingdom

Heal the sick who are there
and tell them, 'The kingdom of God
has come near to you.'

Luke 10:9

And the power of the Lord
was with Jesus to heal the sick.

Luke 5:16-18

The crowds learned
about it and followed him.
He welcomed them and spoke to them
about the kingdom of God, and healed
those who needed healing.

Luke 9:11

Yet the news about him
spread all the more, so that crowds
of people came to hear him and to
be healed of their sicknesses.

Luke 5:15

...and the people all tried to touch him,
because power was coming from him
and healing them all.

Luke 6:19

Great crowds came to him,
bringing the lame, the blind, the crippled,
the mute and many others, and laid them
at his feet; and he healed them.

Matthew 15:30

For this people's heart has become calloused;
they hardly hear with their ears, and they have
closed their eyes. Otherwise they might see with
their eyes, hear with their ears, understand with
their hearts and turn, and I would heal them.

Matthew 13:15

They came to Bethsaida, and
some people brought a blind man
and begged Jesus to touch him.
He took the blind man by the hand
and led him outside the village.
When he had spit on the man's eyes
and put his hands on him, Jesus asked,
"Do you see anything?"
He looked up and said, "I see people;
they look like trees walking around."
Once more Jesus put his hands
on the man's eyes. Then his eyes
were opened, his sight was restored,
and he saw everything clearly.

Mark 8:22-25

I will give you a new heart
and put a new spirit within you.

Ezekiel 36:26

50

He said to her,
"Daughter, your faith has healed you.
Go in peace and be freed from your suffering."

Mark 5:34

Jesus told him,
"Don't be afraid; just believe."

Mark 5:36

He could not do any miracles there,
except lay his hands on a few
sick people and heal them.

Mark 6:5

Filled with compassion, Jesus reached out his hand
and touched the man. "I am willing," he said. "Be clean!"
Immediately the leprosy left him and he was cured.

Mark 1: 40-41

Jesus called his twelve disciples
to him and gave them authority
to drive out impure spirits and to heal
every disease and sickness.

Matthew 10:1

Healing

So they set out and went from village to village,
proclaiming the good news and
healing people everywhere.

Luke 9:6

Heal the sick, raise the dead,
cleanse those who have leprosy,
drive out demons. Freely you
have received; freely give.

Matthew 10:8

They drove out many demons
and anointed many sick people
with oil and healed them.

Mark 6:13

By faith in the name of Jesus,
this man whom you see and know
was made strong. It is Jesus' name and the faith
that comes through him that has completely
healed him, as you can all see.

Acts 3:16

The harvest is plentiful
but the workers are few.
Ask the Lord of the harvest,
therefore, to send workers into
his harvest field.

Matthew 9:37-38

Do you not say, "Four months more
and then the harvest"? I tell you, open your eyes
and look at the fields! They are ripe for harvest.

John 4:35

I sent you to reap what you have not worked for.
Others have done the hard work, and you have
reaped the benefits of their labor.

John 4:38

5

By his wounds
you have been healed.

1 Peter 2:24b

58

Therefore confess your sins to each other
and pray for each other so that you may be healed.
The prayer of a righteous person is
powerful and effective.

James 5:16

"Make level paths for your feet,"
so that the lame may not be disabled,
but rather healed.

Hebrews 12:13

After they prayed, the place
where they were meeting was shaken.
And they were all filled with the Holy Spirit
and spoke the word of God boldly.

Acts 4:31

Crowds gathered also from the towns
around Jerusalem, bringing their sick and
those tormented by impure spirits,
and all of them were healed.

Acts 5:16

The apostles performed many signs
and wonders among the people.

Acts 5:12

...and many who were paralyzed
or lame were healed.

Acts 8:7

He listened to Paul
as he was speaking.
Paul looked directly at him
and saw that he had faith
to be healed.

Acts 14:9

63

Like newborn babies, crave pure spiritual milk,
so that by it you may grow up in your salvation,
now that you have tasted that the Lord is good.

1 Peter 2:2-3

And this is my prayer:
that your love may abound more
and more in knowledge and depth of insight,
so that you may be able to discern what is best
and may be pure and blameless for the day of Christ,
filled with the fruit of righteousness that comes
through Jesus Christ—to the glory
and praise of God.

Philippians 1:9-11

I thank my God every time I remember you.
In all my prayers for all of you, I always pray
with joy because of your partnership in the gospel
from the first day until now, being confident of this,
that he who began a good work in you will carry it on
to completion until the day of Christ Jesus.

Philippians 1:3-6

When I was a child, I talked like a child,
I thought like a child, I reasoned like a child.
When I became a man, I put the ways of childhood
behind me. For now we see only a reflection as in a mirror;
then we shall see face to face. Now I know in part;
then I shall know fully, even as I am fully known.

1 Corinthians 13:11-12

Brothers and sisters,
stop thinking like children.
In regard to evil be infants,
but in your thinking be adults.

1 Corinthians 14:20

In fact, though by this time you ought
to be teachers, you need someone to teach you
the elementary truths of God's word all over again.
You need milk, not solid food! Anyone who
lives on milk, being still an infant, is not acquainted
with the teaching about righteousness. But solid food is
for the mature, who by constant use have trained
themselves to distinguish good from evil.

Hebrews 5:12-14

Therefore, dear friends,
since you have been forewarned,
be on your guard so that you
may not be carried away by the
error of the lawless and fall from
your secure position. But grow in
the grace and knowledge of our
Lord and Savior Jesus Christ.
To him be glory both now
and forever! Amen.

2 Peter 3:17-18

70

I pray that out of his glorious riches
he may strengthen you with power
through his Spirit in your inner being.

Ephesians 3:16

Not that I have already
obtained all this, or have already
arrived at my goal, but I press on
to take hold of that for which
Christ Jesus took hold of me.
Brothers and sisters, I do not consider
myself yet to have taken hold of it.
But one thing I do: Forgetting what is
behind and straining toward what is
ahead, I press on toward the goal
to win the prize for which God has
called me heavenward
in Christ Jesus.

Philippians 3:12-14

...so that you may live a life
worthy of the Lord and please him in every way:
bearing fruit in every good work,
growing in the knowledge of God.

Colossians 1:10

But the fruit of the Spirit is
love, joy, peace, forbearance, kindness,
goodness, faithfulness, gentleness and self-control.
Against such things there is no law.
Those who belong to Christ Jesus have
crucified the flesh with its
passions and desires.

Galatians 5:22-24

74

75

Since we live by the Spirit, let us
keep in step with the Spirit.

Galatians 5:25

Living by

For if you live according to the flesh,
you will die; but if by the Spirit you put to death
the misdeeds of the body, you will live.

Romans 8:13

Lord, by such things people live;
and my spirit finds life in them too.
You restored me to health and let me live.

Isaiah 38:16

the Spirit

Brothers and sisters,
if someone is caught in a sin,
you who live by the Spirit should
restore that person gently.
But watch yourselves,
or you also may be tempted.

Galatians 6:1

The Spirit you received
does not make you slaves,
so that you live in fear again;
rather, the Spirit you received brought
about your adoption to sonship.
And by him we cry,
"Abba, Father."

Romans 8:15

Brothers and sisters,
I could not address you
as people who live by the Spirit
but as people who are still worldly—
mere infants in Christ.

1 Corinthians 3:1

Not by might nor by power,
but by my Spirit, says the LORD Almighty

Zechariah 4:6

The one who
keeps God's commands
lives in him, and he in them.
And this is how we know
that he lives in us:
We know it by the Spirit
he gave us.

1 John 3:24

For those who
are led by the Spirit of God
are the children of God.

Romans 8:14

And if the Spirit
of him who raised Jesus
from the dead is living in you,
he who raised Christ from the dead
will also give life to your mortal bodies
because of his Spirit who
lives in you.

Romans 8:11

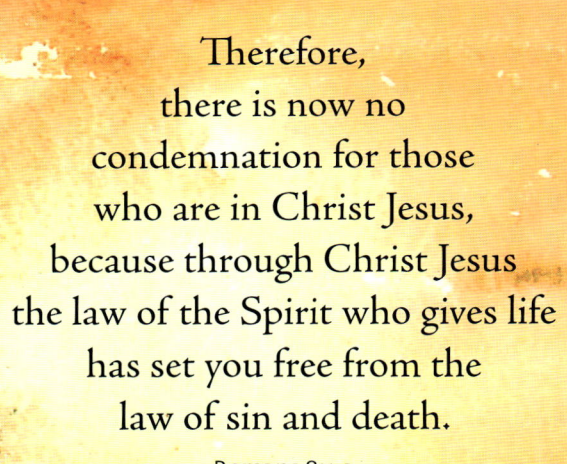

Therefore,
there is now no
condemnation for those
who are in Christ Jesus,
because through Christ Jesus
the law of the Spirit who gives life
has set you free from the
law of sin and death.

Romans 8:1-2

Those who live
according to the flesh
have their minds set on
what the flesh desires; but those who
live in accordance with the Spirit
have their minds set on what
the Spirit desires.

Romans 8:5

The mind governed by the flesh is death,
but the mind governed by the Spirit is life and peace.
The mind governed by the flesh is hostile to God;
it does not submit to God's law, nor can it do so.
Those who are in the realm of the flesh
cannot please God.

Romans 8:6-8

Yet a time is coming
and has now come when
the true worshipers will worship
the Father in the Spirit and in truth,
for they are the kind of worshipers
the Father seeks.

John 4:23

God is spirit,
and his worshipers must worship
in the Spirit and in truth.

John 4:24

But when he,
the Spirit of truth, comes,
he will guide you into all the truth.
He will not speak on his own;
he will speak only what he hears,
and he will tell you what
is yet to come.

John 16:13

I went down to
the grove of nut trees
to look at the new growth in the valley,
to see if the vines had budded or
the pomegranates were in bloom.

Song of Songs 6:11

Riches do not endure forever,
and a crown is not secure for all generations.
When the hay is removed and new growth appears
and the grass from the hills is gathered in,
the lambs will provide you with clothing,
and the goats with the price of a field.

Proverbs 27:24-26

God provides

It had been planted
in good soil by abundant water
so that it would produce branches,
bear fruit and become
a splendid vine.

Ezekiel 17:8

Sow righteousness for yourselves,
reap the fruit of unfailing love,
and break up your unplowed ground;
for it is time to seek the LORD,
until he comes and showers
his righteousness on you.

Hosea 10:12

This is what
the Sovereign Lord says:
"Will it thrive? Will it not be uprooted
and stripped of its fruit so that it withers?
All its new growth will wither.
It will not take a strong arm or
many people to pull it up by the roots.
It has been planted, but will it thrive?
Will it not wither completely
when the east wind strikes it—
wither away in the plot
where it grew?"

Ezekiel 17:9-10

The Lord smelled
the pleasing aroma and said in his heart:
"Never again will I curse the ground because
of humans, even though every inclination
of the human heart is evil from childhood.
And never again will I destroy all living creatures,
as I have done. As long as the earth endures,
seedtime and harvest, cold and heat,
summer and winter, day and night
will never cease."

Genesis 8:21-22

The secret things
belong to the Lord our God,
but the things revealed belong to us and to
our children forever, that we may follow all
the words of this law.

Deuteronomy 29:29

It is to be with him,
and he is to read it all the days of his life
so that he may learn to revere the Lord his God
and follow carefully all the words of this law
and these decrees and not consider himself better
than his fellow Israelites and turn from the law
to the right or to the left.

Deuteronomy 17:19-20a

Celebrate the Festival of Harvest
with the firstfruits of the crops
you sow in your field.
Celebrate the Festival of Ingathering
at the end of the year, when you gather in
your crops from the field.

Exodus 23:16

Six days you shall labor,
but on the seventh day you shall rest;
even during the plowing season and harvest
you must rest.

Exodus 34:21

Celebrate
the Festival of Weeks
with the firstfruits of the wheat harvest,
and the Festival of Ingathering
at the turn of the year.

Exodus 34:22

When you reap
the harvest of your land,
do not reap to the very edges
of your field or gather the
gleanings of your harvest.

Leviticus 19:9

In the fourth year
all its fruit will be holy,
an offering of praise to the Lord.
But in the fifth year
you may eat its fruit.
In this way your harvest
will be increased.
I am the Lord your God.

Leviticus 19:24-25

103

I will make you very fruitful;
I will make nations of you,
and kings will come from you.

Genesis 17:6

As for you,
be fruitful and increase in number;
multiply on the earth and
increase upon it.

Genesis 9:7

God has made me fruitful
in the land of my suffering.

Genesis 41:52b

May God Almighty
bless you and make you fruitful
and increase your numbers until
you become a community of peoples.

Genesis 28:3

"I will increase
the fruit of the trees
and the crops of the field,
so that you will no longer
suffer disgrace among the nations
because of famine."

Ezekiel 36:30

Its leaves were beautiful,
its fruit abundant,
and on it was food for all.
Under it the wild animals
found shelter, and the birds lived
in its branches; from it
every creature was fed.

Daniel 4:12

I will heal their waywardness
and love them freely, for my anger
has turned away from them.

Hosea 14:4

They feast on the
abundance of your house;
you give them drink from your river of delights.
For with you is the fountain of life;
in your light we see light.

Psalm 36:8-9

of healing

Arise, shine;
for your light has come,
and the glory of the Lord
has risen upon you.
For darkness will cover the earth,
and deep darkness the peoples;
but the Lord will rise upon you,
and His glory will appear
upon you.

Isaiah 60:1-2

111

For He who has
compassion on them will lead them,
and will guide them to
springs of water.

Isaiah 49:10

And the lord will continually guide you,
and satisfy your soul in scorched places,
and give strength to your bones; and you will be
like a watered garden, and like a spring
of water whose waters do not fail.

Isaiah 58:11

And the Spirit
and the bride say, "Come."
And let the one who hears
say, "Come." And let the one
who is thirsty come; let the one
who wishes take the water
of life without cost.

Revelation 22:17

Jesus answered her,
"If you knew the gift of God
and who it is that asks you for a drink,
you would have asked him and
he would have given you
living water."

John 4:10

115

You will surely
forget your trouble,
recalling it only as
waters gone by.
Life will be brighter
than noonday,
and darkness will
become like morning.
You will be secure,
because there is hope;
you will look about you
and take your rest in safety.

Job 11:16-18

117

For you will have
the Lord for an everlasting light,
and the days of your mourning
will be finished.

Isaiah 60:20

He has sent me to
bind up the brokenhearted,
to proclaim liberty to captives and
freedom to prisoners....

Isaiah 61:1

Awake, awake...
put on your garments of splendor....
Free yourself from the chains
on your neck.

Isaiah 52:1a,2b

On each side of the river
stood the tree of life,
bearing twelve crops of fruit,
yielding its fruit every month.
And the leaves of the tree are
for the healing of the nations.

Revelation 22:2

Long life to you!
Good health to you
and your household!
And good health to
all that is yours!

1 Samuel 25:6

I will bring health and healing to it;
I will heal my people and will let them enjoy
abundant peace and security.

Jeremiah 33:6

My back is filled with searing pain;
there is no health in my body.
Come quickly to help me,
my Lord and my Savior.

Psalm 38:7,22

I have heard your prayer and seen your tears;
I will heal you. On the third day from now you will
go up to the temple of the LORD.

2 Kings 20:5a

A wicked messenger falls into trouble,
but a trustworthy envoy brings healing.

Proverbs 13:17

...they might see with their eyes,
hear with their ears, understand with their
hearts, and turn and be healed.

Isaiah 6:10b

I have seen their ways,
but I will heal them.

Isaiah 57:18a

"Peace, peace,
to those far and near,"
says the LORD.
"And I will heal them."

Isaiah 57:19b

126

There is a time for everything,
and a season for every activity under the heavens:
a time to be born and a time to die,
a time to plant and a time to uproot,
a time to kill and a time to heal,
a time to tear down and a time to build,
a time to weep and a time to laugh,
a time to mourn and a time to dance,
a time to scatter stones and a time to gather them,
a time to embrace and a time to refrain from embracing,
a time to search and a time to give up,
a time to keep and a time to throw away,
a time to tear and a time to mend,
a time to be silent and a time to speak,
a time to love and a time to hate,
a time for war and a time for peace.

Eccleciastes 3:1-8